AF494939

RAW POETRY

Sharon Ella Tarkington

ISBN-13:
ISBN-10:
ISBN- 979-8-218-21795-2

DEDICATED TO:

This book is dedicated to my beautiful and loving mother Sheryl Dukes. My strong and faithful father Donald Tarkington. My fabulous and special sisters Daylene and Brittany. My protectors and peacemakers, my brothers Donald Jr. "Lil' Don", Richard, and Brandon. My unique and inspiring nieces Jazalynne, Danika, Ella, Brandee J and baby Nova. My fun and ambitious nephews Jaidon and Russell.

God has blessed me to have you all in my life. I would be lost without you guys!! Mom, Dad and Lil' Don know you are walking with us and watching over us. We love you!!

R.I.P XOXO

TABLE OF CONTENTS

CHAPTER 4 - LOVE AND SELF LOVE

CHAPTER 5 – EROTICISM AND KINKY DESIRES

RAW POETRY

CHAPTER 1

FAITH

"Jesus is my hero, He knows I'm a sinner, yet he will always come to save me."

"UNTITLED"

There is no one

To turn to but you God

God

I've been at peace for weeks

I heard that sermon

It humbled me and my soul

But Lord

God

My anxiety is kicking in

I keep telling myself to relax

I'm not sure if it's the demons

Trying to creep inside my brain

All I know is that I want to be a

Better woman of God

God

I wonder with all my sin

Will you still let me in

Into the heavens where

My heart belongs

Oh God

Here I am

I surrender my heart

And soul with the asking

Of forgiveness

You are the Highest Power

"UNTITLED"

"THE ONE AND ONLY GOD"

The spirit of God resides in me

Strong and joyful

I will only come closer to my

God

The one and only

God

As people begin to drift

Out of my life I Know

It's what the Lord has intended

I remain in

My belief and my faith

God is setting up

Something real proper like

Blessings are everywhere I turn

He knows what I need

I just have to be patient

It's hard at times

My mind begins to spin

Round and round

Faster and faster

I feel as though I will drown

Reminding myself

God is the original loyalty

No need to seek it in the flesh

It's ok we are all alike

Full of sin but thirsty

To be Christ-like

It's no reason I should fret

My God

The one

And only

God

Has all authority

I'm not even worthy

Or deserving and

HE STILL LOVES ME!

*"**THE ONE AND ONLY GOD**"*

"NEVER FEAR THE ENEMY"

Being a child of God

Being judged

By the people

As I speak His word

His word

His word

His word is raw and harsh

His word is love and peace

Some wanna ignore the signs

And block out blessings

AAAAHHHH

Go ahead

Look the other way

And let

Sir Lucifer take over

And show you the wrong way

His word

His word is raw

The sins that we commit

On a daily basis

Will be forgiven

It's your choice

God will give you

The choice

Between left or right

You turn left

To shoot up

You turn left

When you turn

Out that trick

You turn left when

A line of snow

Is laid across

The mirror

In your reflection

You see the addiction

But you close

Your eyes

And sniff anyway

You sit back

And pray

He doesn't

Take your life away

I want to give

It all to Him

I see that your struggling with faith

I'm here to send a message

His word

His word

Is gonna be heard

And I'll be

The one to spread it

It will be so

Sweet like honey

Raw honey

Gods words

Are like Raw honey

I push myself

And others

To be more Christ-like

He tests my faith

He questions my hope

He knows and

Understands my trials

That's why

He's given me

A second chance to

LIVE

To live Christ-like

"*NEVER FEAR THE ENEMY*""

"Look at your Hand"

Have you ever had

An outer body experience

Or your flesh and bones

Just doesn't feel real

What if there were

No animals

No humans

No land

Have you ever

Just looked at your hand

And be like

How am I even here

How is it all real

Sober or high

I'm still alive

My body

My life is just my imagination

A God in the universe that controls us all

While I live my life

With guidance of God

He will be the only one

I trust that is real

Even when I feel

As though life isn't real

I look at my hand again

And see that I am real

As real as can be

As well as

Everything around me

Thank you God

For being the realist

"*LOOK AT YOUR HAND*"

"UNTITLED"

Writing is my outlet

The pen and paper

Never judge

I never had

True courage

To recite what

I have written

Because

I was afraid

To be criticized

In my poetry

I am fully me

By expressing myself

Onto the paper

So deeply

It makes it harder

To say it aloud

Encouragement

Has suddenly

Been struck in me

Now

I'm more

Motivated than ever

I'm motivated for

People to hear my words

I want to make

A difference in

Peoples lives

I know that

I can be

Someone else's

Encouragement

As long as I stay

On this ride

I will continue

On this ride and

As long as

I have

God

On my side

I know that

I will Prosper

I know I have

Messages from Him

To those who need it

I just pray

That they will apply it

Apply the message

God

Has sent

And to make a change

God

Has put me

In my place

Writing is my outlet

The pen and paper never judge

The only judge is God above

"UNTITLED"

CHAPTER 2

MENTAL HEALTH AND GRIEVING

"My mind, body and spirit is damaged by the trauma of the heartbreak and pain...

A continuous pain. But I will find a way to cope as long as I have hope."

"DAD'S BOOK"

It will be OK

Once you open this book

You will be OK

It will have

The explanations of why

Why everything has

Happened the way it did

From day one

To the last day

Day one of joy

The last day

Full of pain

Here we are reading

His story

Through our eyes

Oh how there

Are so many regrets

You can't skim

Through the pages

You can't go back

To read it all in depth

Listen to all

Of his lessons

His stories

That only him

And God really know

The universe

And the energy

I feel his presence

I know in my dad's book

He will always

Be a real true hard

Raw smart and

Incredible black man

A black man

With so much strength

And power

A black man with a story

That I wish I could

Read it all in detail

I probably couldn't

Even begin to

Imagine his life

He had to live

He survived through the 60's 70's 80's

Went to war

Where all

He ever did was fight

Fight

For his rights

Fight for my rights

The rights that

Is still being fought for

My dad

His book

Would be so thick

So interesting

You wouldn't even

Want to put it down

Here I am

Reading his

Story through my eyes

I must say

He's my favorite book

"DAD'S BOOK"

"GOD TAKE HER SOUL"

I cant wrap my mind around what is happening

Strokes dementia infection

I.C.U

Oxygen

Oxygen tank

Oxygen needed

God give her

Her own natural oxygen

Your oxygen of healing Lord

Laying in a bed that is not her own

Her rest being interrupted

Throughout the day and night

Praying that healing

Will come around her way

I can't wrap my mind around this hurt

I can't wrap my mind around this pain

How this is happening again

I've continued my faith

In the Lord to reverse

All of her pain

Cure her from all disease

God

As selfish as I like to be

I can't

God knows what he's doing

Being on life support

Her heart lungs liver

Kidneys and everything in

Between is now nonfunctioning

I don't want the Lord to take her

Take her from me

But I know heaven

Is better than life here on earth

So God take her soul

But I beg you Lord to

Leave her heart

And let her spirit be free

"GOD TAKE HER SOUL"

"I'M SUFFOCATING"

Looking in the mirror

But not really looking

Cuz my eyes are closed

I can't see myself

I can't hear myself

I'm suffocating

Where am I

In a building of 4 walls

That I no longer belong to

I'm screaming but no one

Can actually hear me

I can't breathe

Someone

Please

Save me

I don't want to take my life

I can't let my soul

Be damaged anymore

Than it already has

Please let me breathe

Let me open my eyes

Let me out

Or maybe I should Look in the mirror

And ask for the help That my soul

So desperately needs I'm suffocating

"I'M SUFFOCATING"

"NARCISSIST"

Am I victim or survivor of being with a narc

It's like I have a huge sign on me that says

CHOOSE ME!!

Self-centered men and women in my

Life who appear to be lovers and friends

When really they just mirror me

To give us something in common

I'm an empath

But I still fall for that self-admiration

Not even aware of it at first

Being showered with gifts

Compliments and much more

I don't see what's really happening

They craved my attention

And admiration for them which I gave

Which was a major mistake

Here I am still trying to escape

Falling in love with a narcissist

Is extremely dangerous

Self-centered and bratty

I just want to make them happy

So I put up with the abuse

In high hope's it would change

No change

No change at all

No change at all ever

Being friends with a narc

Being in love with a narcissist is shitty

I know what's up now

Except my love is so strong still

Even during the abuse

I chose to be in denial

I choose to be with him

Fuck he's holding me captive

I guess it's time to break free

I just don't want to

Maybe I can make him change

Maybe I can make my friend change

Hahaha

That's the funniest thing I heard all day

"*NARCISSIST*"

"HOW ARE YOU?"

"How are you?" They ask

"How are you?" They ask

Because it's what's polite

My response is something

I don't want to say

Sure I'll let you

Know how I'm doin'

"Right now

I'm goin' fuckin insane

I'm sure later

I will feel the same"

"How are you?"

They ask me

"Oh I'm blessed"

I say

Just so I don't have

To explain my true pain

"Hey Sharon!

Hey! Hey! Hey!

How are you?"

I'm like

"Hey! Hey! Hey!

Hey back!

How am I feeling?

I'm feeling real fake"

Guess what?

I have no happiness

Left in my gas tank

But I'm still driving

The go-go

The go-go

The go-go

That runs on E

E

Empty

Empty in my heart

Empty in my soul

Empty to my core

"How are you?"

"*HOW ARE YOU?*"

CHAPTER 3

THE HUSSTLE LIFESTYLE AND RADICAL

"I used to be ashamed of my past actions. Yet today, I realized those actions I was once ashamed of, IS my testimony. My testimony which I am proud of."

"LIFE OF A FELON"

You wanna know

How it feels like

To be a felon

It's like

Not being human

It's like

Being alien

Always hiding

But still want to be seen

Afraid of getting attacked

Killed

Or becoming

A social experiment

Wanting to shine

And show all the

Pride and success

Unfortunately

At the end of the day

Felons

Get no respect

Felons are humans

And we deserve more rights

The system

Is set up

To make it harder

To stand up

And make a change

For the better

Instead

It has us returning

To the streets

Selling dope

Selling our bodies

Selling our souls

Once again

To the devil

Just to eat

It's just not right

That's what they want from us

A never ending cycle

Of self destruction

Built by

The government

Living the life

Of a felon

Is more like

Being alien

"*LIFE OF A FELON*"

"UNCLE SAM"

We are all toys for them

Little robots

Objects that are controlled

By money greed corruption and brutality

The ones who believe that

They're the owners of the flesh

Of you and I would be

YES

The government

The puppet master

We work sleep and eat

That's all they want us to be

Concerned about

Uncle Sam is the enemy

People are so blinded

To what the predators behind the scenes

Are actually doing

In reality

It's in our faces

In our music

In the cartoons we allow our children to watch

In ALL social media platforms

As the government continues

To play with us

We have no control

They are listening close by in all

Smart fun devices

That no one seems

To be able to put down

We allow our privacy

To be invaded by checking

Yes to the term agreements

Of the apps we download

Makes it easier for them

They yank us by all our parts

Until we fall apart

ITS THEIR PLAN TO SEE US STRUGGLE PEOPLE!

It's their plan for us to sabotage ourselves

Sabotage one another

We get toyed with

We get tortured by

And we get bullied by

Uncle Sam

I'm ready to stand up and say something

Raise my voice

My words will no longer go silenced

FUCK YOU UNCLE SAM!

"UNCLE SAM"

"I DON'T FUCK WITH THE POLICE, THEY FUCK WITH ME"

I don't fuck with the police

They fuck with me

It don't matter where I may be

In the grocery store

Or up the street

Yeah

Even though I'm a good looking woman

When it comes to me all they see is

SHARON TARKINGTON

GET HER

And Got damn I can't even compete

So much in debt with the courts

When really they owe me

I'm entitled to mother fucker!

I still owe for

Disturbing the peace

So what mother fucker

Sure not all police are bad

But bet all the ones I've encountered

Has put me in cuffs one way or another

Three trucks come for backup for little oh me

With only a gram of weed

They want to charge me a few racks

And take away my freedom

Would this had happened

If I weren't black

Loss of work

Bills are passed due

And my mind is so trapped

Now they'll never get their paper

I bet you that

The system is so fuckup

I don't even wanna call 911

When I'm in danger

Because somehow it'll be my fault

I'll be the one in cuffs

I used to like to use handcuffs in bed

Now

It's more like an anxiety attack

I don't fuck with the police they fuck with me

"I DON'T FUCK WITH THE POLICE, THEY FUCK WITH ME"

"HOPELESS HUSTLER"

Up early to get this money

My life consists of feeding

These people what they want

I try to get a day off

And then

RING RING

RING RING

The phone goes off

Movin' from here to there

To get that fast cash

Lookin' over my shoulder

Watchin' clear not to get

Robbed or caught up

By them boys in blue

Stayin up late with barely any food

In my system

I stress because

I need to remain strapped

So tired of counting thousands

Of dollars I can't even keep

I just hand it over like

It's a damn ice-cream cone

Hustlin' for a false dream

Livin' in a nightmare

Wishin' for the day I can live

Without being controlled and pushed

I always say, "Ima get off these streets"

But the money is just too sweet

What else is there for me

"HOPELESS HUSTLER"

"A CAPE MADE OF HOPE"

A cape made of hope

Back in the day when I was a "hoe"

I thought I was invincible

Taken by "surprise"

I was robbed and raped a couple of times

I still wore my cape made of hope

Hope that I would get away

When a trick would tell me

His problems with his wife

I wore my cape

Gave advice and gave him hope

Wasn't always about sex

I had to remind myself

My cape wasn't sewn

To be a captain save a hoe

A cape

My cape

Is made of hope

Hope to save my own soul

He tried to tell me

I was dirty and never

Would make love to me

But had no problems taking the dough

I became a renegade

A cape made of hope

I thought maybe I would be

Better off this way

I looked in the mirror

And decided to be

More than a "hoe"

A cape made of hope

Was made for me

It was made within me

And the life of a hoe

Is hopeless

Especially if you don't

Have your own cape made of hope

Come to me

I will show you how to sew your own cape

Made of hope I promise there is more

"A CAPE MADE OF HOPE"

CHAPTER 4

LOVE AND SELF LOVE

"To love someone fully, you'll need to love yourself fully first. To trust another, you'll need to trust yourself first. Self-love opens the gates to pure love for others. Love should always be kind, true and pure.

"FEMINISM"

Feminism is powerful

Women get taken advantage of on a daily basis

Whether it be in the work environment

In school or even our own home

We provide the womb to carry his child

With no appreciation

Depression tries to take over you and I

It tries to take control over

Strong women like you and I

We refuse to let the devil decide our destiny

Feminism is such a grand movement

It's taking place all over the world

To me that's what we need

Our community counts on us

The young girls that are coming up

Looks up to us

Let's be sure to

Leave the impression needed

For feminism needs to be taken seriously

It's our right as women to be treated equally

Not as if we are wild animals

From across seas with no training

You see

As a unit as a team

As warriors and queens of God

We deserve to be treated equally

We deserve all of what we want and need

No honey

I'm not talking purses and glamour

I mean entrepreneurship

I mean taking a stand for what's

Right and revealing what's wrong

A woman will soon become

Our president of the United States

The United States which has fallen into a mess

She will clean it up

Clean up after the man as usual

After a man has put his doubts in us

All we can do is show him in us

Is more powerful than he thought

Feminism is what will save

Our country and make

Honest changes to the world

That is what God has intended

For the life of a woman

Feminism is phenomenal

We are the missing piece

To the puzzle that a

Man could never understand

"FEMINISM"

"UNMASK YOURSELF"

You want to dismiss others

Out your life to just make room

For another person to

Fill in that space

That space

That should be filled with yourself

Your so codependent

You don't even know who you are

I watch from afar

Shaking my head

Wishing you would take this time

You have to work on yourself

Not he or she

Instead

You mask the silence

You mask the emptiness

You mask what you think is right

All your doing is masking yourself

Masking yourself into destruction

In hopes that the next person will heal you

When in reality your only allowing

More pain to flood your brain

To flood your soul

Shit your losing your sanity

And you don't even know

Being in denial of self worth

You choose to be abused

Because here you are

Still trying to find a way to be amused

It's crazy because when

You look in the mirror

You see yourself

But I guess I wrote

This poem for me

It's really me

The writer

The creator

The one that is trying

To unmask myself

Unmask myself

HELLO!!

It's time to take care of me

Myself and I

It's time to take off the mask

"UNMASK YOURSELF"

"MY BROTHERS AND SISTERS"

My brothers and sisters

What is real respect

What is real respect to you

Please let me know how

Your intellect operates

Seems to operate

In a way that

Is so corrupt

Disrespectful to others

Demanding

Special treatment

From others

After throwing a fit

It's insane

Because you end up

getting what you wanted regardless

Young dudes

Hanging out on the block

With nothing better

To do besides

Harass women

And act like a hawk

Rob and kill

Call one another niggas

My brothers you are not niggas

We are not niggas

We are men and women

Full of beautiful melanin

Oh' my sisters don't act innocent

Because we all know those

Short shorts were worn

To show off that beautiful skin

Then you sit back and cuss

Wonder why

You're treated as a "hoe"

But you my sister

Is not a "hoe"

Never believe

That your attire makes you a "hoe"

All that is

Is the outsiders judging

But my sisters

Just like you call your

Sisters "hoes and bitches"

Is another reason

Why the men believe it's OK

It really doesn't matter then

Now does it

We are embarrassing each other

As the black race

The human race

My brothers my sisters

It all starts

With self-respect

My brothers my sisters

Let's respect ourselves and one another

"MY BROTHERS AND SISTERS"

"UNTITLED"

An intelligent confident

Black woman's perspective

Of seeing the world

In a clear woke vision

Sophisticated glasses rest

On her divine high cheekbones

Regardless her pain

Her smile will always remain

A woman that I'll admire

A lifetime and beyond

My sister my rock

You are my heart

"UNTITLED"

"SELF PEACE IS KEY"

Different energies are

Always trying to get to me

With my peace in it's place

The negative energies try

To get a taste and suck it all away

Protecting my peace is

Protecting me

A beautiful black woman

That can never be beaten

Never taken

Never broken

My peace within me

Is so strong

So powerful that it

Has to be seen

But only if I allow thee

Self peace is key

"SELF PEACE IS KEY"

CHAPTER 5

EROTICISM AND KINKY DESIRES

"Making love. Having sex. Simply fucking whoever is next. It's all the same."

"WATERFALLS"

I don't know you…

With your sexy vibes

With your smooth rymes…

You bring waterfalls

Between my thighs…

I don't know you…

Throbbing inside…

How would you feel inside?

Damn.

As I precum on my legs

No panties on

I keep telling myself

Just rub the clit a little bit

I don't know you

But I want to get to know you

And your shaft

I don't know you

So keep it to yourself

I'm supposed to be celibate

You fuckin me up

I don't know you

But some day I just might

"WATERFALLS"

"POETS DON'T ONLY WRITE ABOUT LOVE AND HEARTBREAK"

Just because I am a poet

Doesn't mean I write

About love and heartbreak

Because I'm a poet

I write about fucking

I fuck you?

Yes

You fuck me?

Yes

But my pen

My pen makes love

To my paper

See I don't love you

So I fuck you

I rather have the pen

In my hand while the

Ink releases all over the paper

Just because I'm a poet

Doesn't mean I only write

About love and heartbreak

I write about how I fuck with

Half my clothes on

But right now

I rather write poetry

Naked

Alone

While on ecstasy

Let the ink and paper

Do all the fucking

And love making to me

Because poets don't only write

About love and heartbreak

"*POETS DON'T ONLY WRITE ABOUT LOVE AND HEARTBREAK*"

"ON THE EDGE"

I'm suffocating

I'm looking over the edge

Scared to jump

My heels are holding me up

As my toes hang over

My heart races every time you

Come around

My mind is wrapped

Around the love making we have

As I ignore the feelings

That linger close to the edge

I'm holding myself back from falling

I know once I jump

There is no turning back

Allowing you to satisfy me

My every physical needs

Yes indeed

You are fully compliant

You are my favorite

Amazed everytime I take a ride

Cumming hard

While you wish you could

Cum inside of me

I wont allow it

I would slip off the edge if I did

I can only give you my affection

I can only provide

My smooth soft skin

And my warm pocket

All I can give to you

Is conversation

Mental connection

My heart cannot exist

Within this scenario

Otherwise

I'll just fall off the edge

Just do as I say

And please my body like you do

But I'm warning you

You just better not fall off the edge

"ON THE EDGE"

"MAKING LOVE TO ME IS LIKE WRITING POETRY"

Making love to me

Is like

Writing poetry

So satisfying and seductive

Marking me with the ink

The ink that easily

Releases onto me

Onto my body

As the poem continues

The plot thickens

My cum thickens

Making love to me

Is like

Writing a fairy tale

Once a princess

Becomes a queen

She runs the palace

The king is just there

To keep her aroused

Happily ever after

After I busted a nut

All over your face

Makin love to me

Is like

Writing an essay

Be sure everything

Is correct

Grammar spelling

Everything in between

I want it to be your very best

I'll be grading your paper

I'll be grading the way you

Play with my clit

And kiss my pussy lips for extra credit

Making love to me

Is like

Writing your heart out

Writing until the ink

Within you has all ran Out

Making love to me

Is like

The best poem you've

Ever written

Because

I'm the best you've

Ever made Love to

Grab your pen and paper

I'll show you how to

Write poetry

Properly

Making love to me

Is like

Writing poetry

"MAKING LOVE TO ME IS LIKE WRITING POETRY"

RAW POETRY

Thank God daily.

Love yourself.

Appreciate others.

Challenge yourself to be the best version of yourself.

Spread love, motivation, and positivity.

ABOUT THE POET

To humbly introduce myself, I am Sharon Tarkington.

My stage name is Tay M.F Digzz. I go by Tay Digzz.

I've been writing since "Once upon of time".

As a kid I would write stories then poetry naturally developed.

I always knew I would be an author.

When I became an adult, I had created thousands of poems over the years.

I pushed myself to get them organized.

I believe "Raw Poetry" was meant to be released when it did.

True life experiences needed to take place.

Writing for me is not only a passion of mine, it is who I am.

Writing is what kept my mental health in check.

Writing is my sanctuary. I can use a sheet of lined paper and pencil

To express my most private thoughts, dreams and fantasies without being judged.

I am able to make a difference in my peoples lives through my writing.

My writing has messages that people need to hear.

In my book "Raw Poetry"

You will find that healing that you've been searching for.

That's what keeps me creating.

9 798218 217952